1741

SCIENCE FILES

TEXTILES

SCIENCE FILES – TEXTILES
was produced by

David West ☆☆ Children's Books
7 Princeton Court
55 Felsham Road
London SW15 1AZ

Designers: Rob Shone, Fiona Thorne, David West
Editor: James Pickering
Picture Research: Carrie Haines

First published in Great Britain in 2001 by
Heinemann Library, Halley Court, Jordan Hill,
Oxford OX2 8EJ, a division of Reed Educational and
Professional Publishing Limited.

OXFORD MELBOURNE AUCKLAND
JOHANNESBURG BLANTYRE GABORONE
IBADAN PORTSMOUTH (NH) USA CHICAGO

05 04 03 02 01
10 9 8 7 6 5 4 3 2 1

ISBN 0 431 14304 8 (HB)
ISBN 0 431 14310 2 (PB)

British Library Cataloguing in Publication Data

Parker, Steve, 1952 -
Textiles. - (Science files)
1. Textile fabrics
I. Title
620.1'97

Printed and bound in Spain by Bookprint, S.L., Barcelona

PHOTO CREDITS :
Abbreviations: t-top, m-middle, b-bottom, r-right,
l-left.

Front cover - tl, 4b & 28m (Rosenfeld Images Ltd),
br & 8tr (Ed Young) - Science Photo Library. bl, 3 &
2lr (Charlie Westerman) - Robert Harding Picture
Library. bm & 12bl - Spectrum Colour Library. 5b &
29b (Bildagentur Schuster), 6l (Bildagentur
Schuster/Eckstein), 8bl (Jeff Greenberg), 9tl
(Schuster), 9tr (Duncan Maxwell), 11bl (Adam
Woolfitt), 14br, 15bl (Occidor Ltd), 15br (G & P
Corrigan), 20t (J.H.C. Wilson), 23t (Bildagentur
Schuster/Bramaz), 29tr (J. Legate), 13mr, 18bl, 26t -
Robert Harding Picture Library. 6/7 (John Eastcott &
Yva Momatiuk), 9bl (Jack K. Clark/Agstock), 9br
(Carlos Munoz-Yague/Eurelios), 11tr (Philippe
Plailly/Eurelios), 16l inset (Debra Ferguson/Agstock) -
Science Photo Library. 5tr, 7r, 15tr, 16tr, 23br - Mary
Evans Picture Library. 10bl & tr, 10/11 (Richard
Waller), 12tr (Nick Gordon), 13tr (François Gohier),
13br, 14bl (Wardene Weisser) - Ardea London Ltd.
11br, 14tr, 22t, 27tr - Ann Ronan Picture Library.
11tl (M. Ryan), 21tl - Spectrum Colour Library.
19bm & br - Culture Pavilion. 13tl (Peter Jefferies) -
British Camel Association. 28bl - DuPont

*An explanation of difficult words can be
found in the glossary on page 30.*

SCIENCE FILES

TEXTILES

Steve Parker

Heinemann
LIBRARY

CONTENTS

Many items of clothing are still cut out and stitched together by skilled workers rather than by machines. The exact shape of the garment can be varied to suit the type of cloth, and the way it stretches over or drapes from the body.

INTRODUCTION

Long ago, someone felt cold, and invented clothes. The first items of clothing were probably cloaks of furry animal skins. By 7,000 years ago, people were weaving together animal hairs, or strands of plant fibres, to make sheets of cloth – the earliest textiles. Today, textiles are a huge world industry. Cloths, fabrics and materials are not only used to cover our bodies and keep us warm. They are made into curtains, rugs, seat and furniture covers, and also used in planes, cars, powerboats, hi-tech sports equipment, vehicle tyres, spacecraft – in fact, almost everywhere.

Spinning and weaving were once done by hand. Machines like this power loom from 1862 greatly speeded the process.

The past one hundred years has seen the invention of many artificial (man-made) fibres, such as nylon, acrylic and polyester.

Artificial fibres make special fabrics for sport clothing. They are lightweight, stretchy and very smooth, to slip speedily through the air.

NATURAL FIBRES

Textiles are made from fibres or filaments, which are long, thin and bendy. Natural fibres come from plants and animals. Flax, cotton, wool and silk are types of fibres that have been used from ancient times.

FIBRE FEATURES

Fibres for textiles should be flexible, so that they can bend for weaving or similar processes. The fibres should be long and strong, so the textile does not fall apart or tear too easily. And they should be long-lasting, so it does not rot away or crumble.

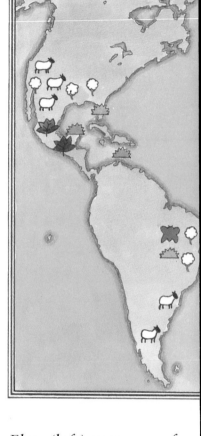

Flax (left) was one of the commonest plant fibres, used to make linen cloth. However, it was largely overtaken by cotton in the 1800s.

Different breeds of sheep (below) provide wool with differing features and qualities.

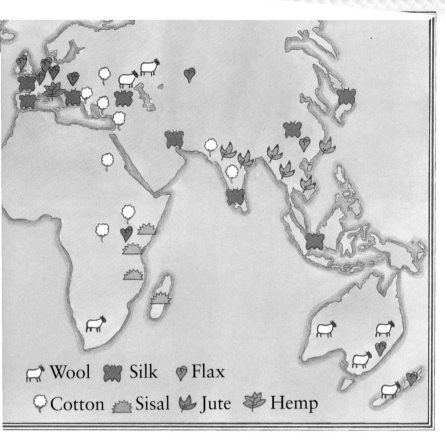

Wool   Silk   Flax
Cotton   Sisal   Jute   Hemp

Each region of the world produces different natural fibres. This depends partly on which plants grow in the climate and soil, and which animals are kept. It also depends on customs and traditions. In Ancient China, the origin of silk fibres was kept secret until silkworms were smuggled to the Middle East, in the year 552 BC.

Facts from the PAST

Most natural fibres are stretched out and twisted together, to make long lengths of rope-like yarn or thread. This is known as spinning. In Ancient Greece, spinning was a relaxing pastime for rich ladies.

MORE FIBRE FEATURES

The fibres for textiles also have special features which they pass on to the fabric made from them. Silk is very smooth and slippery. Sheep's wool is curly and springy, and traps air between the fibres, for warmth. Much thicker, stronger natural fibres from certain plants are used to make string, twine, ropes and mats.

COTTON AND FLAX

In the textile industry, the most common natural fibre is cotton. Most of the T-shirts, socks, pants, knickers and towels in the world begin as cotton plants.

HAIRY SEED PODS

Cotton fibres come from the part of the cotton plant called the boll or seed-head. They are white and fluffy, with fibres 2–3 centimetres long. The fibres are mixed up with cotton seeds and must be separated from these by a process known as ginning.

Cotton plants take 4–6 months to produce ripe bolls. These are picked by harvesting machines.

Ginners separate fibres from seeds.

GINNING COTTON

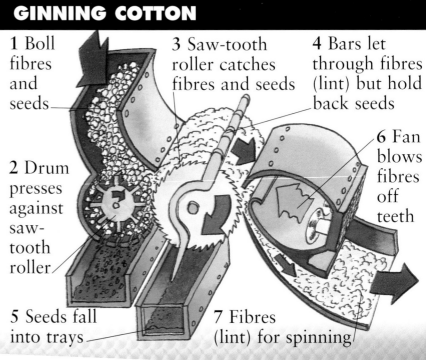

1 Boll fibres and seeds

2 Drum presses against saw-tooth roller

3 Saw-tooth roller catches fibres and seeds

4 Bars let through fibres (lint) but hold back seeds

5 Seeds fall into trays

6 Fan blows fibres off teeth

7 Fibres (lint) for spinning

FLAX

Flax fibres are from the plant's stalk or stem. The plants are harvested by machines or by hand. The stalks are retted, or soaked in water, for several days or weeks. Then they are dried, beaten and scraped, and combed or hackled, to release the long fibres.

Flax plants are grown for the long fibres in their stems, and also for their seeds. The seeds are squashed or pressed to release their oil, known as linseed oil.

After drying, flax stems are beaten, and scraped or scutched, to loosen the long fibres within the stems.

Bales of ginned cotton fibres, ready for spinning.

The cotton gin separates fibres from seeds and other bits of boll. It also helps to clean and comb the fibres, which are packed into bales. The first cotton gin was invented by Eli Whitney in 1793–4. Modern versions work in much the same way. Cotton seeds are used for vegetable oils, margarines, soaps and as animal foods.

Ideas for the FUTURE

The fibres of cotton bolls are white. But one day, they may be any colour you wish. Cotton plants could be changed by genetic modification, GM. This would reduce the need to dye or colour the fibres later.

GM cotton: which colour today?

OTHER PLANT FIBRES

Several kinds of plants have strong, stringy fibres used for making textiles. The fibres are obtained by various methods such as shaking, soaking and scraping, similar to flax (page 9).

JUTE AND SISAL

Jute is a tall plant up to 3.5 metres high. The fibres come from under the bark-like skin. They are long, thick and coarse, and used for sacking, bags, ropes, carpet backs and linings. Sisal fibres come from this plant's leaves. They are also coarse and used for ropes, brushes and rough cloth.

Each leaf of the sisal plant contains more than 1,000 fibres, up to 1.5 metres long. Their uses include ropes and cords.

Jute is grown mainly in India and nearby countries. The stems are soaked in water, dried and crushed to loosen and separate the fibres.

Jute is loaded for boat transport to the spinning factory. Its fibres are fairly weak and brittle, and do not take up dyes well.

Kapok bushes will grow to several metres high.

KAPOK AND HEMP

The light, fine, fluffy fibres of kapok are found on the tree's seed pods. They are used for stuffing and padding. Hemp fibres come from the plant's stem. Their main uses include bags, sacking, ropes and rough canvas.

Fibres of the hemp bush are removed and dried in a similar way to flax fibres. They are up to 2.5 metres long, tough and long-lasting.

Most fibres are stretched and twisted into yarn or thread in the same way, by spinning.

This is a jute spinning factory. Jute is one of the longest natural fibres, up to 3 metres.

Facts from the **PAST**

Hemp resists water and rotting. It was made into hammocks, ropes, strings and cords for old sailing ships. Today, like many other natural fibres, hemp has been largely replaced by stronger artificial (man-made) fibres.

Hauling on a hemp rope, 1881.

Wool is the soft, wavy fur or hair of sheep. It is the commonest animal fibre used for textiles.

WOOLLY FEATURES

Wool fibres are soft and stretchy. They absorb liquids like sweat and dyes well. They can be washed clean and spring back into shape. These features make wool an excellent textile fibre.

Sheep are 'dipped' regularly in a bath of strong chemicals. These kill pests on the skin, such as fleas and lice.

A sheep's woolly coat, or fleece, is snipped off by hand. This is known as shearing. It is done using scissor-like shears or electric clippers.

WHAT IS WOOL?

Wool is similar to your hair and the fur of other animals. It is made of keratin, a protein substance. Each fibre grows at its living base, from a tiny pit in the skin, called a follicle. The main shaft of the fibre is made of millions of microscopic cells and is quite dead.

Rod-shaped cells of cortex (inner layer)

Flat, scaly cells of cuticle (outer layer)

WOOL FIBRE

lpacas have
een shorn for
ool for
enturies.

TYPES OF WOOL

The finest wool comes from the Merino and Rambouillet breeds of sheep. Other animals also produce wool-like fibres. These include camels in Africa and Asia, and their cousins the alpacas, vicunas and llamas in South America. Breeds of goats raised for wool include the Angora and Kashmiri. The finest wool comes from the under-coat, which is beneath the tough, coarse-haired outer coat.

Uses of camel-hair range from coats to tents.

Mohair cloth is made from Angora goats' wool.

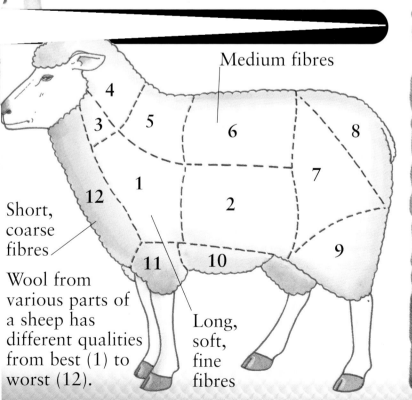

Medium fibres

4

3   5

6   8

7

1

12   2

Short,
coarse
fibres

11   10   9

Wool from
various parts of
a sheep has
different qualities
from best (1) to
worst (12).

Long,
soft,
fine
fibres

Ideas for the FUTURE

Sheep-shearing is a skilled and tiring job. In the future, we could have a new breed of sheep – the self-shearer! All of its wool would fall out naturally when the sheep was fed a certain tablet. Like on sheep shorn normally, the fleece would quickly grow again.

Shiver time – but wool soon regrows.

Silk makes some of the softest, smoothest, yet strongest of all fabrics. It has been greatly valued since ancient times.

THE SILK-'WORM'

Silk is different from other animal-produced natural fibres. It is not curly, wavy or crimped (kinked). It is in the form of very long, smooth, thin filaments, made by silkworms. These are not real worms. They are the larvae or caterpillars of a pale-winged, furry-bodied moth called the silk moth.

Facts from the **PAST**

Silk may seem delicate, but its filaments are as strong as the artificial fibre nylon. The idea of making cloth from the filaments of the silkworm cocoon first arose in China about 2600 BC.

This print shows a silk-clad worker gathering mulberry leaves to feed the caterpillars.

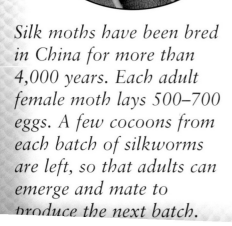

Silk moths have been bred in China for more than 4,000 years. Each adult female moth lays 500–700 eggs. A few cocoons from each batch of silkworms are left, so that adults can emerge and mate to produce the next batch.

A WORM'S LIFE

The silk moth develops like other moths. The adult (1) lays tiny, pale eggs. Each hatches into a small silkworm (2), which eats mulberry leaves (3) for five weeks. It spins a case or cocoon (4), and becomes an inactive pupa or chrysalis (5). Two weeks later the adult emerges.

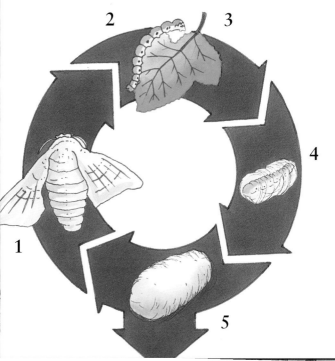

The best silk is used to make very costly garments. This advert from the late 1920s also shows the silk moth, caterpillar and cocoon!

la
SETA NATURALE
è vero lusso

LONG, STRONG

A silkworm spins its cocoon from a single filament up to 1,500 metres long. Cocoons are sorted into different grades of quality and softened in hot water. A filature machine combines several filaments into one thread of raw silk, which is wound on to a reel. Several threads may be interwoven to make silk yarn thick enough for weaving.

Silkworms eat only fresh mulberry leaves (left). When they have spun their cocoons, these are collected and sorted (above).

Silk filaments are so thin that more than 20 may be wound and twisted, to make a thread or yarn called raw silk.

The first artificial or man-made fibre was produced in the 1880s. In fact, though its fibre was artificial, the substance it was made from was natural – wood!

RAYON

The artificial fibres known as rayons are based on cellulose. This is found in great quantities in wood. The wood is pulped and mixed with chemicals to obtain the cellulose. This is further treated and squirted through tiny holes to make long, smooth fibres called filaments.

This 1929 advert shows the smooth, silky qualities of rayon.

Cellulose is one of the main substances in wood and in many other plant parts, such as cotton fibres.

MAKING RAYON

1 Cellulose sheets soaked

2 Sheets fed into shredder

3 Shredded pieces left to 'age' in bath of caustic soda

Cellulose comes mainly from wood, especially unwanted chips and bits from sawmills. The chips are soaked in a bath of chemicals to make them soft and separate out the cellulose. This is pressed into sheets ready for the rayon process.

4 Carbon disulphide mixed in

5 Mix is churned into lumps

6 Mix dissolves to form pulp

Viscose rayon is made by mixing cellulose with caustic soda and carbon disulphide. Its filaments are ideal for heavier cloths and fabrics. A similar process using the chemicals copper oxide and ammonia produces finer filaments for silk-like fabrics.

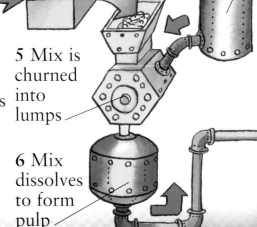

ARTIFICIAL SILK

The first types of rayon were invented as a more available, and less costly, form of silk. At first they were called 'artificial silk'. But in 1924, producers of the filaments agreed to call them rayon. Today the various types of rayons make up about one-fifteenth of all artificial fibres. They have many uses, from elegant clothes to the strong, net-like webbing inside motor vehicle tyres.

Rayon soaks up, or absorbs, liquids well. It is used for medical dressings and chemical filters.

The size of the spinneret's holes (below) affect the thickness of rayon filaments. They can also be stretched even thinner by jets of water.

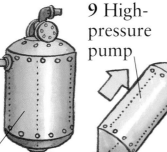

Rayon filaments are very long, smooth, straight, and all the same thickness.

Ideas for the FUTURE

The cellulose for rayon is obtained mainly from wood, which means cutting down trees. A tree of the future may grow fibres of cellulose on the outside rather like a stick of celery. These could be stripped off and used straight away.

Celery has a fibrous outer layer.

9 High-pressure pump

12 Filaments are stretched and wound on to reels

11 Filaments go solid in acid bath

7 Filter press turns mix into thick liquid

8 Settling tank removes air bubbles

10 Liquid mix is squirted through spinneret holes

Following rayon (see page 16), scientists tried to make totally artificial fibres, from mixtures of chemicals. They succeeded in 1938 – and have been making more ever since.

NYLON

The first fibre made completely from laboratory chemicals, rather than from natural substances, was nylon. It was an instant success, both for fashionable clothing and for military and industrial uses, like parachutes and strengthening cords in tyres. There are now dozens of artificial fibres. Many are types of plastics, such as polyester and acrylic, made from petroleum.

At the refinery, petroleum (crude oil) is separated into hundreds of substances. Some of these go to make artificial fibres.

Labels show that many items of clothing that seem natural are made from combinations of artificial fibres.

Aramid artificial fibres do not rot in sea water.

1 Mix is made stronger by evaporator

2 Oven heats mix to form nylon

3 Melted nylon oozes on to casting wheel and cools solid

4 Solid nylon is crushed into chips

5 Chips are mixed with hydrogen and melted

6 Liquid is forced through spinneret holes and cooled by air fan

Raw nylon mixture

7 Nylon fibres are spun and wound on spool

Computer

Cooling water

Nylon begins with a mix of chemicals such as adipic acid and hexa-diamine, from the chemical factory. A series of changes involves more chemicals, heat and pressure. Filaments are produced like those of rayon, by squirting out of tiny holes in a spinneret. Nylon was successful for several reasons. It could be woven as very smooth, thin, light but strong fabrics, which were easy to wash and dry. It did not rot or go mouldy when damp, so armed forces soon used it for parachutes, tents and similar equipment. In the 1960s nylon took over from wool as the main fibre in carpets.

Facts from the **PAST**

Nylon was developed in the 1930s at the Du Pont Chemical Company, by a team led by Wallace Carothers. He had the idea that small units or molecules, called monomers, could be joined end-to-end, to form giant molecules known as polymers. These were long enough to form fibres.

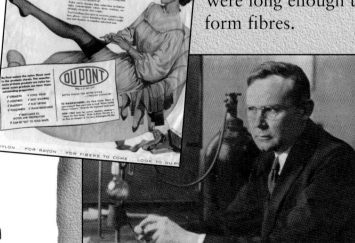

Wallace H. Carothers (1896–1937).

Natural fibres such as wool and cotton are too short to weave, sew or knit. So the fibres are made into very long threads or yarns, by spinning.

ROLL AND TWIST

The main idea in spinning is to twist or twirl together many short fibres, so that they overlap each other, and interlock with enough strength that they cannot slide past each other. Typical cotton fibres are about 2–3 centimetres long. At any place along a piece of cotton thread, almost one hundred fibres are twisted together.

Before spinning, fibres such as cotton must be drawn several times, by sets of rollers. This makes the fibres slide past each other so that they are all in line, or parallel, without bends, kinks and knots.

CARDING

A natural fibre such as cotton is matted and mixed with unwanted bits, and must be prepared before spinning. In carding, the fibres are pulled past tiny wire hooks which tease and comb them into a strip, the sliver.

DRAWING

Next, several slivers pass between pairs of rollers. The first pair turn slowly, the next pair faster and so on. The slivers are drawn, or stretched lengthways and merged together, so their fibres lie more alongside each other.

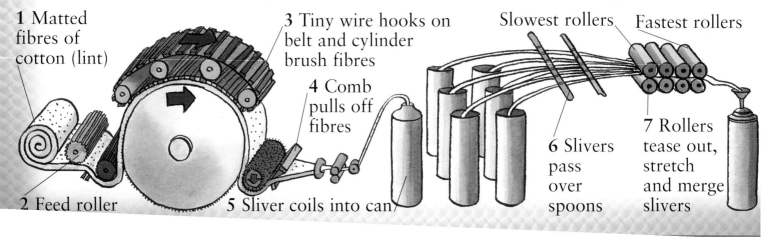

1 Matted fibres of cotton (lint)

2 Feed roller

3 Tiny wire hooks on belt and cylinder brush fibres

4 Comb pulls off fibres

5 Sliver coils into can

Slowest rollers   Fastest rollers

6 Slivers pass over spoons

7 Rollers tease out, stretch and merge slivers

Facts from the **PAST**

Until the 1200s, threads were hand-spun using a whorl and spindle. From the 1300s the spinning wheel greatly speeded the process. The 1700s saw a series of powered spinning machines: the jenny, frame and mule. With powered weaving looms, textiles became much less costly. *A traditional spinning wheel being demonstrated.*

A spinning machine must wind the yarn or thread at high speed and very neatly, on to a reel, spool or bobbin. It can then be fed off again into a high-speed weaving loom.

SPINNING BY AIR

The exact process of spinning depends on the types of fibres and their length, strength and stretchiness. In open-ended spinning, blasts of air pull fibres into a fast-spinning cup and make them line up parallel, as the cup twists them into yarn.

ROVING

Roving is like the first stage of spinning. More rollers turn at increasing speeds to stretch the sliver. The strands then pass down the hollow arm of a spinning flyer, and twist as they are fed on to a sliding bobbin.

SPINNING

The first-stage yarn, called roving, is once again drawn out, so its fibres are straighter and parallel. Then they are fed through a small sliding loop, the traveller, and twist naturally as they wind on to the bobbin.

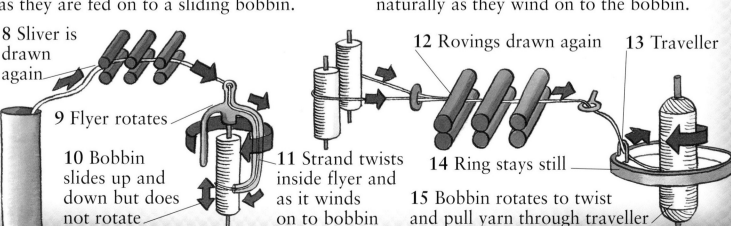

8 Sliver is drawn again

9 Flyer rotates

10 Bobbin slides up and down but does not rotate

11 Strand twists inside flyer and as it winds on to bobbin

12 Rovings drawn again

13 Traveller

14 Ring stays still

15 Bobbin rotates to twist and pull yarn through traveller

'Textile' comes from an ancient word which means 'to weave'. This involves passing yarns under and over each other.

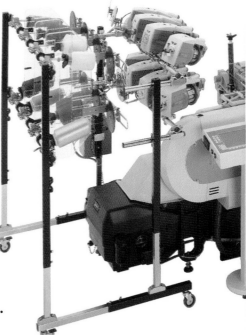

The Jacquard loom of 1805 used large cards with holes in them to produce woven patterns. It was an early automatic machine.

FIRST WEAVERS

Weaving was perhaps invented for making baskets and nets, out of long vines and plant stems. In most textile weaving, one set of yarns is interlaced with another set, by threading them under and over each other. This was once done by hand. Today, most weaving is by machines called power looms.

WEAVING ON A LOOM

A loom has two sets of yarns or threads. Warp yarns lay lengthways, neatly in line, close together. The weft yarn feeds out of a small, pointed shuttle, as it passes sideways between the warp yarns. For one pass of the shuttle, even-numbered warps (2, 4, 6 and so on) are lifted while odd-numbered warps (1, 3, 5 and so on) are moved down, by frames or shafts. Then the warp yarns are reversed, with evens down and odds up, so the shuttle can go the other way. And so on, and on.

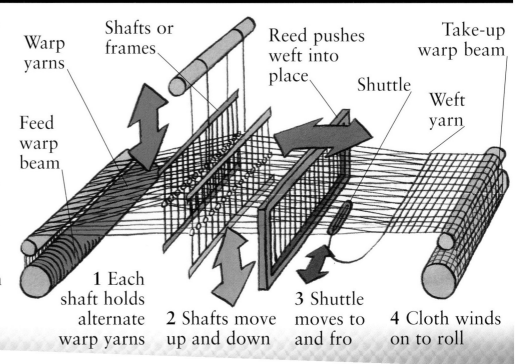

Warp yarns

Shafts or frames

Feed warp beam

Reed pushes weft into place

Shuttle

Take-up warp beam

Weft yarn

1 Each shaft holds alternate warp yarns

2 Shafts move up and down

3 Shuttle moves to and fro

4 Cloth winds on to roll

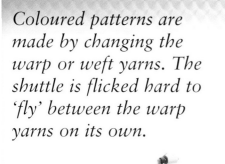

Coloured patterns are made by changing the warp or weft yarns. The shuttle is flicked hard to 'fly' between the warp yarns on its own.

For a smooth fabric, the warp and weft threads must be spaced evenly. They must also be under equal tension – pulled by the same amount. The loom operator examines the cloth regularly, and counts the number of warps and wefts in a certain distance, to check all is well.

WEAVING EFFECTS

There is a huge number of different weave patterns. Thin yarns close together produce a close-weave fabric, while increasing the gaps makes it more open-weave. Bath-towels (terry towelling) have two sets of warp or weft threads. One set makes the flat part of the cloth, the other set forms the raised loops.

TYPES OF WEAVE

Plain weave with one warp for one weft

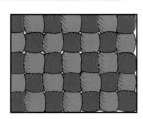

Twill weave where the weft goes under two warps each time

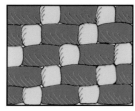

Two thin warps with one thick weft

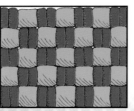

Facts from the PAST

Like spinning, weaving was once done solely by hand. Simple looms were in use by 5,000 years ago in Europe and Asia. A great step forward came in 1733 when John Kay invented the 'flying shuttle'. The shuttle was thrown or flicked between the warp yarns, by a device called a picker, unwinding weft yarn as it went. This was faster than pushing it by hand.

A loom from the 1860s.

At one time, the word 'textile' meant only woven fabrics. Today it includes fabrics and cloth made by other methods.

KNITTING

In knitting, a single length of yarn is used as both warp (lengthways) and weft (crossways). The knitter makes a series of knots, called stitches, by linking together loops of yarn using long, thin knitting needles or a machine.

After weaving, knitting is the second most frequently used method of fabric manufacture. Banks of knitting machines (above) cope with countless varieties of yarns and patterns.

Weft (purple)

Warp (green)

In a knit stitch, the loops are pulled to the front of the fabric (the side that shows). In a purl stitch (above), they are pulled to the back.

Ideas for the **FUTURE**

Some substances are able to take in or absorb heat quickly, then give it out slowly, bit by bit. Could these substances be added to yarns of the future? You could pop your coat into an oven. Later, as it slowly gave out heat, it would keep you warm for hours.

FELTING

A woven textile has fibres and threads neatly arranged in patterns. A felted material does not. Its fibres are jumbled up at random. The fibres are usually pressed hard, and heated, perhaps with small amounts of glue-like chemicals, so that they mat together with each other. Unlike woven cloth, which has lines and ridges, felts are the same in every direction.

Felt is used on pool and snooker tables, where the balls must roll evenly in any direction. A tennis ball has felt with thicker fibres.

FINISHING

Some textiles are treated to give a certain 'finish'. Different finishes are used for appearance, to prevent creases or snags, to make the fabric more water-resistant, and for many other reasons. In singeing, the surface fibres are heated so they burn very slightly.

A simple type of finish is brushing, where fibres at the surface of the cloth are loosened and made to lie in the same direction, as a pile. Napping is similar but more severe, as tiny hooks pull out and tease some of the fibres. Lustre is a very smooth, shiny finish.

SINGE

NAP

LUSTRE

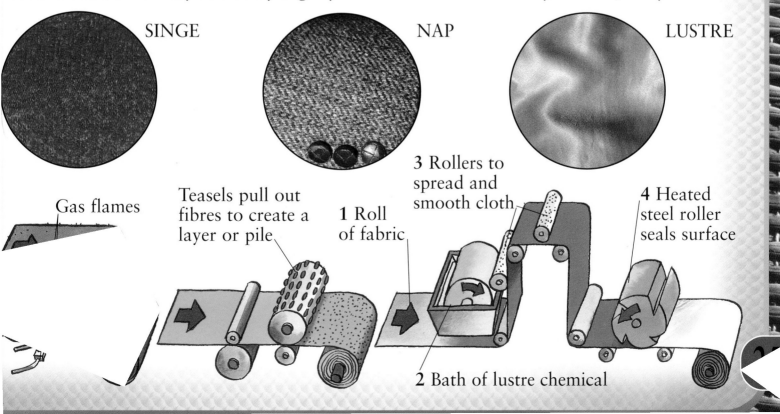

Gas flames

Teasels pull out fibres to create a layer or pile

1 Roll of fabric

3 Rollers to spread and smooth cloth

4 Heated steel roller seals surface

2 Bath of lustre chemical

DYES AND PRINTS

Some textiles are left untreated. They are the colours of their original fibres. But most textiles are coloured in some way, using dyes and prints.

PRINTING

Prints are pictures, words and designs put on to a finished garment, fabric or other item, using coloured inks. There are many methods of printing. Ink may be pressed on to the fabric from a wooden or metal block, or by a revolving roller.

SCREEN PRINTING

In this type of printing, ink is pushed or squeezed through tiny holes in a screen, on to the fabric. A stencil or mask stops ink passing through to parts where it is not wanted on the fabric. The screen may be made of fabric itself (originally it was silk) or very thin wire mesh. As in most methods of printing, different colours of ink are applied separately, one after the other, to build up the complete picture or pattern.

Roller printing puts inks on to textiles at hundreds of metres per minute.

Screen in tray   Ink trough   Stencil or mask   Roller pushes ink through screen

1 First colour is screen-printed on to cloth

2 Second colour is screen-printed on to cloth

3 Inks are dried

DYEING

A dye is a strongly coloured substance, or pigment, usually in a liquid such as water. Textiles can be dyed at any stage, from the original fibres to the finished item, by soaking in the dye. Different fibres, both natural and artificial, take up and hold dyes in various ways. For example, rayon dyes very well, but jute does not. Often yarns are dyed different colours, then woven into a fabric in a certain order, to produce coloured patterns such as stripes.

William Perkin (1838–1907).

In tie-dyeing, fabric is knotted or tied tightly with string. The dye cannot soak evenly into all parts.

A transfer has heat-sensitive inks on a backing sheet. Heat from the iron melts the inks and they soak into the fabric.

Carpet-weavers can produce very complex designs. Some of their methods still remain secret.

Making textiles is a long and complex process, from original fibres to finished item. Many people are helping to develop new textiles, such as chemists who invent new kinds of artificial fibres, and weaving experts who devise new ways of putting them together.

There are increasing numbers of permeable or 'breathable' fabrics, such as Gore-Tex. They allow moisture to pass through one way only. When used for clothing, they let sweat from the skin get out, but they prevent wind and rain coming in. Most of these fabrics have several layers. They are used especially for outdoor and survival clothing.

Kevlar is used for bullet-proof clothes, almost unbreakable ropes, windsurfer sails and hang-glider wings.

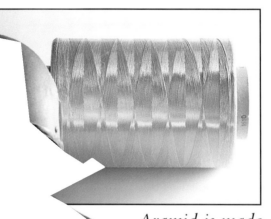

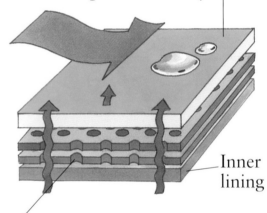

Weatherproof outer layer

Inner lining

Aramid is made as long, smooth filaments.

Micro-pores (tiny holes) allow moisture to pass one way only.

STRONGER THAN STEEL

Some artificial or synthetic fibres are stronger than steel strands of the same size. Aramid has a chemical structure which is similar to nylon, but this fibre has even greater strength and resists heat, chemicals and physical knocks. It is woven into lightweight, ultra-tough, tearproof fabrics such as Kevlar, with many specialized uses.

RECYCLING TEXTILES

Clothes, curtains, carpets and other textile-based items cost millions to make, both in raw materials and in machinery and fuels. It is very important to re-use or recycle fabrics, especially by taking unwanted items to a clothing collection point or 'rag bank'. The fibres can be pulled apart and separated, and used again to make felts, padding, cleaning pads and similar products.

Clothes may be used again, or processed into cleaning rags, dusters and other items.

COMBINING FIBRES

Most textiles are made by traditional spinning and weaving. But modern technology allows fabric designers to put together fibres in many new ways, such as winding one type of fibre around another. Twisting fibres tightly like corkscrews means that they can uncoil and stretch easily, up to ten times their normal length.

Non-stretchy fabric

Stretchy fabric

Fibres can be combined in various ways for different purposes.

Smooth, stretchy fabrics like Lycra make ideal sportswear.

TEXTILE CHART

	TYPE OF FIBRE	FEATURES AND USES
ANIMAL	Wool (from sheep and other furry animals)	Very adaptable, springy fibres, can be spun and woven in many ways, absorb moisture, keep in warmth; used for all kinds of clothes, blankets, carpets, insulation and many other products
ANIMAL	Silk (from silkworm caterpillars)	Very long, smooth, thin, strong filaments; used for high-quality clothes, sheets, stockings, scarves, linings, tapestries
PLANT	Cotton (seed pods or heads of cotton plant)	Short, fluffy fibres spin and weave well, hold dye, absorb sweat and moisture, wash well, dry quickly; used for all kinds of clothing and underwear, bedding, towels, pads, medical items
PLANT	Flax (from stem)	Long, flexible fibres are not very stretchy; used to make sewing thread, nets and twine, and woven into linen fabric for clothing, drapery, tablecloths, napkins and similar other items
PLANT	Sisal or agave (from leaf)	Long, strong, stiff, coarse fibres; used for rough cloth, bags, ropes, string, brushes
PLANT	Hemp (from stem)	Long, strong, stiff, long-lasting fibres; used for sacks, bags, rough canvas, ropes and twine
PLANT	Abaca (from leaf stalk)	The strongest leaf fibre, also called Manila hemp; used mainly for 'cordage' – rope, string, twine, cord and cable
PLANT	Jute (from stem)	Very long fibres, but coarse, brittle and difficult to dye; used for sacks, ropes, carpet backing, mats and rough lining
ARTIFICIAL	Rayon/viscose (from plant cellulose)	Very long, smooth filaments, absorb moisture and dye well, adaptable in strength and softness; used for clothes, drapery, pads, filters, reinforced or strengthening webs and nets
ARTIFICIAL	Nylon	Very long, smooth filaments, varied in strength and softness, resists damp, rot and chemicals; used for clothing, bedding, covers, drapery, ropes, string, fishing line, nets, reinforcements
ARTIFICIAL	Acrylic (propenoic acid, type of plastic)	Fibres can be made soft, fluffy and 'fleecy'; generally used in a similar way to wool
ARTIFICIAL	Polyester	Hollow fibres are used for warm clothing, padding and lining

GLOSSARY

cellulose
A substance which makes up large parts of plants, including wood, fibres and the thick walls of microscopic plant cells.

dye
A coloured substance or pigment, usually spread out or dissolved in a liquid such as water or a solvent.

filament
A fibre or strand of material that is very long, smooth and straight, yet flexible.

ginning
Separating the fibres from the seeds and other parts of the cotton plant's seed head (boll).

permeable
Able to be permeated (passed through) by liquids or gases.

polymer
A very large chemical grouping or molecule, made from many smaller units (monomers) joined together.

retting
'Rotting', soaking parts of a plant such as flax to loosen the fibres.

shearing
Clipping or snipping the fleece from a sheep or similar wool-bearing animal.

spinneret
A nozzle or knob with tiny holes, through which liquid is squirted, to become filaments or fibres.

synthetic
Artificial or man-made – something that is not found in nature.

warp
Yarns or threads that lie lengthways in a woven fabric, with the weft threaded sideways, up and down between them.

weft
Yarns or threads that lie crossways in a woven fabric, with the warp threads passing lengthways, up and down between them.

INDEX